Original title:
Tropical Nights, Moonlit Skies

Copyright © 2025 Creative Arts Management OÜ
All rights reserved.

Author: Seraphina Caldwell
ISBN HARDBACK: 978-1-80581-482-5
ISBN PAPERBACK: 978-1-80581-009-4
ISBN EBOOK: 978-1-80581-482-5

The Night's Velvet Cloak

Under stars that wink and tease,
A raccoon steals my spring roll with ease,
The moon giggles from high above,
While crickets sing of lost love.

Palm trees sway like tipsy friends,
Mangoes dance as laughter blends,
Coconuts drop with thudding grace,
Cheeky turtles join the race.

Lanterns of the Isle

Bright lanterns sway, a quirky sight,
As glowworms dance, oh what a night!
The flamingos strut with flair and style,
While parrots squawk and crack a smile.

In the sand, a party's begun,
With sea turtles mixing, oh what fun!
A sea breeze whispers secrets near,
While everyone chugs coconut beer.

Velvet Tides and Silvery Shores

Waves crash in a bubbly roar,
As moonbeams bounce on the ocean floor,
A crab in shades throws a quick jig,
While the dolphins show off their big gig.

Seashells giggle, buried in sand,
As sandy toes refuse to stand,
Starfish plan a late-night feast,
Forget the lines—just dance like a beast!

Call of the Nightbirds

Nightbirds chirp a funny tune,
As owls hoot at the bright balloon,
While fireflies flicker like clumsy stars,
Dressed in outfits made from candy bars.

Laughter spills from dusk till dawn,
As raccoons wear hats, ever drawn,
With mischief ready, joy in the air,
The night is wild—let's not despair!

Beneath the Glowing Tides

Sandy toes at midnight's call,
A crab shows off, he thinks he's tall.
Dancing shadows chase the moon,
Is that a fish that just went 'Boom!'

Laughter echoes on the shore,
Did the tide just slam the door?
A starfish joined our silly game,
While dolphins laugh, we feel the same.

Celestial Serenade in a Coastal Haven

The stars play hide and seek tonight,
A parrot squawks, it's quite a sight.
With coconuts as our fine drink,
We toast to stars and dolphins' wink.

A hermit crab joined in the cheer,
He wears a shell, it's quite sincere.
The breeze teases with salty air,
While fish gossip without a care.

Night's Mosaic of Silver and Gold

Twinkling lights dance on the wave,
A coconut laughs, oh how we crave!
The moon attempts a flashy dive,
While clams debate how best to thrive.

The sand's our stage, with shells our props,
A critter show until it stops.
A splash too loud brings quite a fright,
"Is that a shark?" Not quite, just light!

Breathe of Seafoam in the Starlight

Whispers travel on the breeze,
Is that a crab playing with keys?
The waves go 'splash' as we all cheer,
Bringing fish tales we long to hear.

A jellyfish floats by with grace,
We giggle hard, it makes a face.
Underneath the stars' great glow,
The laughter rises, ebb and flow.

Tranquil Nightfall

The crickets chirp a lively tune,
While lizards dance beneath the moon.
A frog leaps high, a daring stunt,
He lands quite soft, oh what a hunt!

The palm trees sway with silly glee,
As if they're doing the cha-cha, you see.
A friendly breeze that tickles the face,
Whispers secrets of this crazy place.

Ballad of the Breeze

An errant feather floats on by,
Caught in a gust, it starts to fly.
A coconut drops with a loud thud,
It missed my head, thank goodness—phew, what a dud!

The stars above play hide and seek,
As if they're giggling, oh so cheek.
Each twinkling light winks with delight,
While waves crash softly—what a sight!

Gaze Upon the Abyss

I stared into the vast, dark sea,
And felt a fish nibble at my knee.
It swam away with quite the flair,
Leaving me laughing, gasping for air!

The shadows dance upon the shore,
As sand crabs scuttle and explore.
I hoot and holler, join their fun,
In this wild realm, I'm never done!

Enchantment Beyond the Horizon

The tiki torches flicker and sway,
As if they want to join the play.
A parrot squawks a terrible joke,
Causing nearby cacti to choke!

A hammock sways—a cozy nest,
But watch out, it may be possessed!
I tumble over, land with a grin,
Counting the stars, let the fun begin!

Night's Canvas Painted in Light

The stars are like sprinkles on a cake,
As crabs do the cha-cha beside the lake.
With laughter that echoes from tree to tree,
Even the owls are dancing with glee.

A coconut falls, it gives a loud thud,
Releasing a splash, it makes quite a flood.
The moon winks, as if it knows the game,
And fishes below are never the same.

Whispers of the Sea and Starry Fairytales.

The fish tell jokes, a real swimming spree,
While jellyfish bounce like they're on a spree.
Crabs wear sunglasses, looking quite cool,
And dolphins surf on waves as a rule.

Seagulls squawk loudly, they're comedians,
Trading old tales with all their fans.
Stars giggle softly, knowing the fun,
As the night grows old, but never is done.

Whispers of Dusk

The sky blushes pink, quite absurdly bright,
While fireflies flicker like stars taking flight.
Bats swoop and dive, but they wear a grin,
Pretending they're actors in a big spin.

A parrot recites a poem so grand,
To a pineapple that's close at hand.
Laughter erupts as the sun waves goodbye,
Leaving night's secrets in the star-speckled sky.

Celestial Embrace

The moon plays tag with the clouds up above,
While crickets perform in the dance of love.
A manta ray floats, wearing a bright hat,
As the sea becomes a stage for a cat.

With coconuts shaking, they join the parade,
As the stars nod along, the night's prank is played.
Everyone chuckles beneath the great dome,
In this grand ballet, we all feel at home.

Silhouette of the Evening Tide

The coconut crabs dance with glee,
As the parrotfish swim wild and free.
Under palm leaves, we sway and spin,
Trying to catch the seagulls' grin.

A boat sails by, tipped with a cap,
The captain's snoring—what a mishap!
We throw him coconuts as bait,
He wakes with a start, oh isn't life great?

Darkened Horizons and Distant Calls

The frogs croak jokes, they crack us up,
While the fireflies swarm like a buzzing pup.
A pineapple falls, what a sight to see,
Rolling away like it's trying to flee!

The moon peeks in—shh, don't give away,
Our secret dance party for a fun Saturday.
But wait! Who's that with the goofy move?
It's just the cat trying to groove!

Night's Enchantment

Amidst the chatter of crickets and cheers,
We share our laughter over colorful beers.
A lizard whispers, 'I love your shoes,'
We laugh so hard, we're blowing some fuse!

Beneath the stars, we plan a parade,
Of dancing bananas and coconut trade.
The night echoes back our playful schemes,
As we chase our dreams in hilarious themes!

Dreams Beneath Starry Canopies

With skies adorned in twinkling lights,
We listen closely to the owl's flights.
It hoots a riddle, we try to guess,
But only end up in a silly mess!

Playing limbo with a garden hose,
While the turtles cheer with their slow-paced toes.
We giggle and tumble, what a delight,
As the night wraps us in its funny insight!

Veils of Evening

The parrot squawks a tune, so bright,
While crabs dance sideways, what a sight.
Frogs in tuxedos croak and sing,
As tourists giggle at everything.

The hammock sways, the coconut falls,
A lizard sneaks in, causing some brawls.
With drinks in hand, we toast the day,
And laugh till the stars begin to play.

Glow of the Night Lantern

The lanterns flicker with a wink,
While fireflies outshine every drink.
A cat in a hat sneaks past the light,
Chasing shadows, oh, what a fright!

The beach ball rolls, it takes a dive,
Right into the waves, it does survive.
With sand in our toes and smiles galore,
We giggle and tumble, who could ask for more?

Serenity in the Sway

While sipping juice from a pineapple cup,
A monkey steals snacks, then slurps it up.
Palm leaves rustle, like whispers of cheer,
As seagulls squawk, "What's for supper, dear?"

The surfboards wobble, the kids all yell,
One kid falls off; oh, how he fell!
But laughter erupts; it's all in the game,
Under the stars, we're all just the same.

The Pulse of the Evening Breeze

The breeze tickles noses, a cheeky tease,
As we play charades with the buzzing bees.
A coconut's dropped, right on a toe,
And laughter erupts like a sparkling show.

Bongo drums beat, legs start to sway,
Dance like no one's around, hip-hip-hooray!
With sandwiches flying, a picnic's in flight,
We'll laugh 'til the sunrise chases the night.

Moonbeams and Mango Trees

Under a moonbeam's glow,
Mangoes begin to sway.
The parrots sing a tune,
While the monkeys shout hooray!

Lime green lizards dance about,
On a breeze that's quite a thrill.
They wear tiny sunglasses,
And climb up the mango hill.

A coconut drops with a thud,
Right on a snoring toad,
He dreams of surfboard riding,
As he burbles down the road.

When the stars come out to play,
We'll join the funky beat.
With a fruit hat on our heads,
We'll bust a move, so sweet!

Dreams on the Seashore

Waves whisper jokes to the sand,
As sea turtles roam free.
A crab with shades scuttles by,
Singing, 'Come dance with me!'

Seagulls gossip overhead,
Trading tales on the wing.
While the starfish play poker,
In a game that's quite the fling.

A jellyfish floats like a boss,
Waving its fancy frill.
It tries to dance but trips,
In a plunge that gives a thrill!

Sandcastles lean to the right,
Looking quite out of whack,
But the kids just keep on laughing,
As the tide pulls them back.

Enchanted by the Night

Fireflies hold a rave,
In the garden lush and bright.
They blink their tiny lanterns,
In a most peculiar sight.

A frog croaks a hip-hop beat,
With style that's quite the feat.
While flowers sway their petals,
To the rhythm oh so sweet.

The moon wears a silly grin,
Twirling clouds all around.
While owls hoot disco tunes,
This night's a joy unbound!

Crickets join the dancing fun,
With tiny tap shoes on,
As we twirl under the stars,
Till the break of dawn is drawn.

The Sway of Silent Palms

Palms sway like they're groovin',
With the breeze as their DJ.
They chuckle at lost hats,
In a playful, breezy way.

Coconuts drop, and we jump,
In a comical surprise.
While the waves roll in with laughs,
As the sun begins to rise.

The sand tickles our toes,
In a game of hide-and-seek.
We search for shells and treasures,
While the crabs play hideique.

Finally, we collapse and smile,
As the warmth takes us ends,
Under the sway of the palms,
With laughter, bliss, and friends!

Under the Canopy of Stars

Beneath the bright celestial glow,
A lizard dances, putting on a show.
It slips and slides without a care,
While sipping cocktails, I just stare.

The parrots squawk in wild delight,
While I fumble with my very first bite.
A coconut falls and starts to roll,
I laugh so hard, it takes its toll.

My friend claims he can see a face,
In every star in this vast space.
I squint and nod, then burst out loud,
These cosmic jokes sure draw a crowd!

The moon winks down, a cheeky sprite,
As we giggle and take flight.
In this jovial, starlit dome,
Who knew the jungle felt like home?

Lullabies of the Ocean Breeze

The waves sing softly, splashing near,
While crabs do the cha-cha, oh what a cheer!
A seagull steals my salty snack,
Then squawks and flutters, but I won't crack.

The breeze brings whispers, tales of old,
A mermaid's secret, or so I'm told.
I check my hair, it's a frizzy mess,
But hey, who cares? I'm living in jest!

Sandcastles rise, then tumble down,
As I build a throne, my sandy crown.
The tide rolls in, a playful foe,
I wave goodbye to my royal show!

So grab your floaties, let's ride the wave,
And dance like no one's watching – be brave!
In the evening glow, life's such a tease,
With lullabies sung by the ocean breeze.

Serenade of the Night Bloom

The flowers giggle, petals aflame,
Each one laughing, playing a game.
Bees buzz around like they're in a race,
Trying to find the best hiding place.

A gecko croons a funky tune,
While frogs join in beneath the moon.
They harmonize, their voices collide,
Creating a sound where magic hides.

I tiptoe past with quiet delight,
And trip on roots that twist and bite.
Who knew flowers could dance and sing,
While I just try not to trip on a thing?

So here I am, a festive plight,
Amongst the laughter of the night.
With every bloom, I feel the craze,
In this riot of scents and frolicsome ways.

Shadows in Paradise

The palm trees sway like they've got moves,
While shadowy shapes engage in grooves.
I swear I saw a dance-off commence,
With monkeys aiming to prove their finesse.

The crickets chirp a cheeky beat,
While I attempt to tap my feet.
A butterfly flutters in fancy flight,
Spreading giggles in the soft moonlight.

The tiki torches start to sway,
As fireflies join the bright ballet.
I stumble over roots and grass,
And laugh at how I am such an ass.

So join the fun, embrace the night,
With shadows laughing in sheer delight.
In paradise, no worries remain,
Just joy and jests, a blissful refrain.

Starlight and Silhouettes

Under the bright and quirky moon,
Dancing shadows sing a tune,
Coconuts sway without a care,
Palm trees laughing in the air.

Crabs in tuxedos do a jig,
While fireflies flash like a light-brig,
The sea breeze tickles all around,
As giggles echo, joy is found.

A mango falls and starts to roll,
It bounces up, a fruity goal,
A parrot jokes in colors bold,
As tales of the night gently unfold.

So grab your hat and join the fun,
With every beat, we're never done,
In this parade of silly sights,
Where laughter reigns through starry nights.

Nocturnal Dreams

In midnight's grasp, a dreamer snores,
While mangoes tumble, roll on floors,
A gecko whispers jokes so bright,
As laughter dances through the night.

A turtle races just for laughs,
While sipping on some fruity drafts,
In a caper of oddball delight,
Dreams create mischief in moonlight.

The whispering breeze plays tricks on hair,
Jellyfish pirouette with flair,
Crickets play tunes, a circus show,
Nocturnal antics in a row.

From pink skies down to sandy toes,
A trampoline made of blooms and bows,
In this carnival of sounds and beams,
Everything's funny in nocturnal dreams.

The Rhythm of Palm Fronds

Palm fronds sway like salsa dancers,
Tickling noses, prompting stances,
With every gust, a giggle flies,
In the sway of fun, no one's shy.

Moonbeams drip like honey sweet,
Fluffy clouds perform a beat,
The stars twinkle at this boisterous show,
With hidden jokes, they steal the glow.

A samba of laughter fills the air,
As parrots try their own flair,
In this raucous symphony we find,
Palms and personalities intertwined.

So let your toes dig in the sand,
And join the dance, go hand in hand,
Because here beneath the gleaming stars,
The rhythm guides us, no need for cars.

Midnight in a Sunlit Land

The clock strikes twelve, the antics start,
   Where sunlit dreams play their part,
   A hermit crab spins tales so grand,
   He wears a shell and makes a stand.

Laughter erupts with every breeze,
   Jelly beans rolling with such ease,
   In this land of playful delight,
   Every shadow hides a joke in sight.

The ocean giggles, surf's so cheeky,
As surfboards float on waves so sneaky,
   With coconut drinks that never spill,
   The party's alive, it's a riot, a thrill!

So let's toast to this friendly spree,
While stars take turns to dance and spree,
   In a land where sunsets never end,
Good vibes and laughter, our perfect blend.

Calls from the Moonlit Jungle

In the jungle, critters groove,
Swaying limbs in rhythmic move.
Monkeys swing with silly grace,
While parrots dance and make a face.

The fireflies blink like disco lights,
Frogs croak tunes that reach great heights.
A sloth in shades lounges with flair,
Claiming he's the king of air!

A snake slides down to judge the beat,
Hissing softly, tapping feet.
With rhythm fresh, the nights unfold,
As laughter echoes, bold and gold.

Under stars, the fun ignites,
Tarzan learns to tango, oh what sights!
The moon is grooving, bright and clear,
Join the party, bring a cheer!

Revelry in the Quietude

In the quietude of night's embrace,
A squirrel sports a party face.
With acorns piled like little treats,
He hosts a bash, all critter beats.

The owls are DJing, wise and chill,
While raccoons munch on snacks at will.
A chorus of cicadas hums along,
As crickets croon their night-time song.

A tortoise races, he's quite the sight,
Moving slow but full of might.
"Catch me if you can!" he gleefully moans,
While laughter echoes in leafy tones.

Under boughs, the fun won't cease,
With whispered tales of mischief and peace.
Nature's club thrives with delight,
In revelry that lasts all night!

The Lure of Evening Colors

As the sun dips low, the hues transform,
Pink and orange swirl in a warm swarm.
A lizard sips on nectar sweet,
While a parrot prances, tapping feet.

The flamingoes flaunt their vibrant flair,
Strutting across with a silly air.
They stilt and tease, a vibrant ballet,
While frogs wish they could join the display.

An iguana wearing shades looks cool,
Says he's the best of the school.
With laughter echoing in the boughs,
He winks and bows, the king, he vows.

In vibrant realms, the night takes hold,
With shades of laughter, bright and bold.
Creatures gather, a joyful sight,
In evening's colors, pure delight!

Rhapsody of Nightfall

In nightfall's rhapsody, tales unfold,
Where critters gather, brave and bold.
A goat with a hat sings off-key,
Claiming he's the next big marquee.

The raccoon's juggling sticks and stones,
While the hedgehog plays on ancient phones.
They laugh and cheer for every flub,
In this wild, laughter-packed hub.

A gopher sells tickets to the show,
With a creaky laugh, he's the star, you know.
They tap dance under the twinkling glow,
With every misstep, the laughter flows.

As night wraps all in its cozy shawl,
Creatures unite at the grand hall.
In rhapsody of joy, they sing and play,
Under starlit skies, they dance away!

Shadows Dance on Sandy Shores

Beneath the palms, shadows prance,
They twist and twirl, what a funny dance!
Crabs take a bow, then dash away,
While seagulls squawk, in their own ballet.

The beach ball giggles, rolls away fast,
Chased by a toddler, who trips at last.
Sandcastles crumble, oh what a sight!
As waves come in, claiming the night.

Luminous Dreams in Island Air

With fireflies sparkling, the night's alive,
A lizard sneaks, thinking it can thrive.
Coconuts chuckle, from high in a tree,
While monkeys swing, shouting, 'Look at me!'

Laughter erupts from the beachside grill,
As hot dogs fly, what a messy thrill!
An island breeze dances through the night,
Disguised as a prankster, it's pure delight.

Echoes of the Ocean's Embrace

Waves whisper secrets, they giggle and play,
As shells join in, they'd like to sway.
A fish in a bowtie, swimming with glee,
Says, 'Come join my party, there's room for three!'

The starfish boogie, performing so grand,
While octopuses juggle with shells in hand.
It's a splash party, everyone swims near,
Just don't ask the dolphin to volunteer!

A Soiree with the Celestial

Stars take their places, with a wink and a glance,
They giggle in chorus, inviting a dance.
The moon pulls a prank on the night's soft glow,
"Catch me if you can!"—then it moves slow.

Clouds wear their costumes, fluffy and bright,
While comets zoom past in a playful flight.
A cosmic confetti flies through the air,
Who knew the universe could be so rare?

Crickets' Serenade

In the garden, crickets sing,
With their chirps, they dance and swing.
Each note a joke, a silly pun,
Under the glow, their laughter's fun.

Frogs join in, they croak and play,
Trying to steal the show today.
With each ribbit, a punchline's found,
In this concert that knows no bound.

Fireflies wink in time with beat,
Joking lanterns, what a treat!
Who knew bugs could hold a show?
Making us giggle, it's quite the glow.

So listen close, the night is bright,
With laughter echoing in the night.
In this arena of jest and cheer,
Nature's comedy, loud and clear.

Secrets of the Midnight Sea

Waves chuckle softly on the shore,
Whispers of fish and tales of yore.
Jellyfish dance in shimmery gowns,
While the crabs in tuxedos prance around.

The octopus has painted arms,
With colors bright, it flaunts its charms.
Seahorses giggle, tails entwined,
In their underwater show, oh so refined.

Starfish plot with great delight,
To juggle seashells, what a sight!
Clownfish honk with their bright red clown,
In this aquatic circus, they never frown.

So dive beneath where the pranks unfold,
In the midnight blue, stories told.
The ocean's secrets, spun with glee,
Make a splash in funny jubilee.

When the Stars Descend

Stars tumble down like sprinkles of joy,
Falling from skies, oh what a ploy!
They land in gardens, slick and neat,
Turning the flowers into a treat.

Moonbeams sneak in wearing a hat,
"Did you miss me?" they ask the cat.
Glowing bright with a twinkle of sass,
In this goofy show, they're first in class.

The night owl hoots a riddle or two,
While the raccoons throw a wacky boo!
Silly shadows play hide-and-seek,
As laughter rings through realms mystique.

So when the stars drop, don't you frown,
Join the revelries twirling around.
For in this ballet of giggles benign,
Every sparkle's a joke, divine!

Aroma of Night Blossoms

Fragrant petals whisper, 'Smell me here!'
While honeybees buzz with a buzz of cheer.
The jasmine giggles in the evening air,
With secrets of sweetness, everywhere.

Moonflowers yawn and stretch so wide,
"Wake me up when the fun's outside!"
In the jasmine breeze, they sway and spin,
Join the party, let the night begin!

Moths flutter by, in capes of gray,
Chasing the scent, come join the play!
With every twirl, they fluff and swoon,
In this fragrant gala beneath the moon.

So take a whiff, let laughter bloom,
In the garden's dance, dispel the gloom.
For in these blossoms, pure delight,
Lies a world of giggles, through the night.

Mysteries Unveiled by the Tides

Crabs dance sideways, quite the show,
Their tiny legs move, 'look at me go!'
The seaweed whispers, 'I'm not a snack,'
While the fish all giggle, 'It's quite the knack!'

Seashells gossip, but who can hear?
A clam's wild tale brings everyone cheer.
The dolphins play tag and make quite a fuss,
While seagulls squawk, 'Please, don't blame us!'

Waves crash with laughter, a tickle fight,
Surfboards wobble, hold on tight!
Even the moon grins, what a surprise,
As surfboards surf by with mischievous eyes!

The tide pools bubble, a comedic scene,
Starfish are arguing, they're not so keen.
The ocean's a stage, the night's the cue,
With laughter and splashes, oh what a view!

Reflections of Light on Gentle Waves

The water winks at the silver glow,
As fish wear sunglasses—'How do we flow?'
A penguin slides in, so slick and proud,
Grabbing a drink, he shouts, 'I'm loud!'

The coconut drinks are stacked real high,
While crabs in tuxedos wave goodbye.
Palms sway gently, they've lost their hats,
As a hermit crab struts, 'Hey, check my mats!'

The moonbeam laughs, doing the twist,
While turtles join in, they can't resist.
A sea cucumber says, 'What's this fuss?
I'm just a veggie, don't bother us!'

Light shimmers softly, dances in place,
While clownfish pose with a silly face.
The waves keep rolling, a giggling spree,
In this watery world, who could disagree?

A Night's Portrait of Palm Fronds

Palm fronds wiggle, a funky dance,
A squirrel joins in, takes a silly chance.
The night is alive with parties galore,
As frogs croak tunes, 'Let's dance some more!'

Flamboyant flowers don colorful hats,
While lizards parade with silly spats.
The crickets play music, pitch out of tune,
But the fireflies flash, sharing the moon!

A monkey swings by, quite the acrobat,
With a cheeky grin, it shouts, 'Look at that!'
Coconuts chuckle, spilling their juice,
While the wind hums softly, a light-hearted ruse.

Stars twinkle brightly, a comic show,
As shadows dance freely, putting on a glow.
It's a night full of giggles, oh what delight,
In nature's grand gallery, everything's bright!

Harmony of Stars and Salt

Stars sprinkle salt in a cosmic stew,
While the ocean giggles, 'Hey, how are you?'
The waves murmur secrets, oh what a tale,
As jellyfish shimmer, setting the sail.

The crabs have a meeting, plotting a game,
While seagulls swoop down, just looking for fame.
'What will we do with this starry night?'
'How about a party?' 'Oh what a sight!'

A wise old turtle gives sage advice,
'Bring snacks and drinks, maybe some spice.'
He winks at a shrimp with a pearly grin,
'Let the fun begin, let's haul everyone in!'

The surf sings a song, the night's serenade,
With echoes of laughter, an endless charade.
Under the stars, life's a magnificent spell,
In this saltwater realm, all's well that ends well!

The Calypso of Evening's Glow

Under stars that wink and tease,
A coconut spills, oh what a breeze!
The monkeys dance, full of glee,
While roaches waltz with tangy brie.

The palm trees sway, they lose control,
A parrot sings, a raucous role!
With laughter loud, the tide does play,
As crabs proclaim their fine buffet.

A fisherman dreams of fish so grand,
But hooks a flip-flop, on the sand.
With every wave, the ocean hums,
While seagulls squawk of lost gum.

The night blooms bright with jokes to share,
A party starts, beyond compare!
Though the moon may tease with silver beams,
It's the laughter that fuels our dreams.

Chasing the Echo of Night's Dream

In shadows deep, the iguanas race,
One trips and falls, oh what a face!
They chase each other, full of flair,
While crickets offer tunes to share.

A firefly sparks with comic zest,
A silent giggle in its quest.
While frogs croak loudly, what a show,
As turtles join in, moving slow.

The beach is alive with echoes of fun,
A dance party started, oh, what a run!
With sand between toes and laughter grand,
A coconut bowl, where drinks are planned.

But in heels too high, a girl takes flight,
She lands in a tide pool, what a sight!
But everyone bursts into cheering sound,
As fish join in, the merriment found!

Secrets of the Dusk's Allure

As night unfolds its velvet cloak,
The crabs engage in a fine joke.
With tiny hats, they strut and sway,
While the moon throws light on their ballet.

The breeze is soft, it tickles the skin,
While a lost flip-flop begins to spin.
The laughter gets caught by the breeze,
As owls hoot in muffled tease.

A pineapple float drifts near the bay,
With party hats, it leads the way.
Mango-scented voices lift the vibe,
As starry winks form a glow tribe.

A coconut drinks from a straw so neat,
While seabirds join for a scanty treat.
Together they sing of the night so bright,
In this blissful, giggling, silly flight!

A Tapestry of Shadows and Glows

Amongst the palms, the shadows dance,
While the frogs contemplate their chance.
A lizard struts with a silly hat,
While crabs do the limbo, imagine that!

The ocean whispers tales of old,
Fishes gossip, oh what a bold!
With every splash, a joke unfurls,
As mermaids giggle, their hair in swirls.

A beach ball rolls with a cheeky bounce,
While a watermelon sings, the crowd pronounced!
Chasing dreams in the moon's soft beam,
As laughter echoes by the silver stream.

The night drapes fun in layers thick,
While a pastry floats, wobbly and slick.
A party of shadows, with giggles that grow,
In this enchanted realm, the mirth will flow!

Stars, Shadows, and Samba

Under the stars, a dance appears,
Samba beats evoke youthful cheers.
The shadows sway, a funny sight,
Tripping over toes in the moon's light.

Laughter echoes across the sand,
As clumsy couples take a stand.
The sea gives sighs, it's in on the joke,
As wave after wave, the rhythm they stoke.

With twinkling moments in their eyes,
They leap and spin, their giggles rise.
Even the palm trees start to groove,
Feeling the energy, they too want to move.

At midnight, the moon gives a wink,
As friendships form and emotions link.
In this wild party, under the night,
Even the sea creatures join in the delight.

Hushed Litanies of the Shore

The waves whisper secrets, soft and low,
While seagulls laugh, putting on a show.
In sandy robes, they strut with flair,
Underneath the twinkling, starry glare.

The crabs dance sideways, a comic line,
With fancy moves and sparkling brine.
Shells echo giggles from sandcastle kings,
Hearts light up with the joy that it brings.

Whispers mingle with the night breeze,
As palm fronds laugh with delightful ease.
The beach seems to chuckle at its own fun,
As everyone dreams 'til the rise of the sun.

With waves as their stage and stars above,
The shore holds tales of giggles and love.
In this serene night, a funny encore,
A celebration of life on the shore.

Luminous Love Letters

Under the moon's soft, shimmering glow,
Lovers pen letters that dance to and fro.
With laughter and giggles, words filled with glee,
As they scribble 'I love you' in the sand by the sea.

The crickets serenade, but here's the twist,
They all bring their friends to add to the list.
Each note gets a twist, a rhyme or a pun,
Even the stars get in on the fun.

With hearts on their sleeves, they play with delight,
Crafting tales of romance in the starry night.
The sea rolls its eyes, as the tales grow tall,
While shells giggle softly, just enjoying it all.

Each letter shines bright, under the moon's dive,
Full of humor and joy, where love comes alive.
In this secret world, all worries take flight,
As laughter and love fill the endless night.

Reflections on a Silver Sea

Reflective waters sparkle like dreams,
The silver sea dances with mischievous beams.
Fishes don hats and twirl with flair,
The waves giggle softly, a whimsical air.

Beneath the surface, the jokes float around,
As playful dolphins leap up from the ground.
Shells carry tales of a comical crew,
Grinning at antics of the evening view.

With every splash, laughter does rise,
As sea turtles roll, to everyone's surprise.
They tell tall tales of the big fish they've caught,
While crabs play charades, each gesture a plot.

In this moonlit hour, where the sea comes alive,
All creatures unite in this quirky jive.
Each twinkle and ripple, a humorous breath,
Celebrating life, with no fear of death.

The Scent of Blossoms at Dusk

The flowers bloom, oh what a sight,
As bees dance round in sheer delight.
They've had too much honey, it's plain to see,
Buzzing like they've drank too much tea.

The fragrance wafts, it tickles the nose,
While crickets chirp their silly prose.
They sing their tunes, a wild serenade,
While I try hard to avoid the cascade.

Laughter spills forth like a waterfall,
As I trip on roots, oh, hear my call!
The petals swirl, they cover my shoes,
Now I'm the clown with floral blues.

Under the stars, we twirl and tease,
With nature's perfume on the evening breeze.
So let's enjoy this wondrous jest,
As blossoms bedazzle, I must confess!

Ciphers Written in the Sand

Footprints dance upon the shore,
Each one giggles, begging for more.
Ciphers etched in grains so fine,
I swear this one reads, 'Buy me wine!'

Waves crash in, a sly little prank,
As my secret messages begin to tank.
Written love notes, now soggy and wet,
I should've used leaves, now I regret!

Seagulls squawk, what nonsense they spew,
"Are those hieroglyphs, or just dried goo?"
I scratch my head, it's all in the past,
Like my beachball ideas—none seem to last.

Yet still I write, with hope and glee,
Maybe a treasure map—just for me!
At least the tide keeps me in check,
As I scribble on sand, what the heck!

Dreamscapes Beneath the Night's Embrace

In dreamland's grip, the sails unfurl,
As my ice cream drips, what a swirl!
Unicorns prance in pajamas so bright,
I laugh out loud at this glorious sight.

Clouds made of marshmallows float on by,
While fish in tuxedos swim through the sky.
I chase after giggles, can't catch a one,
In a realm where reality comes undone.

Pineapple hats on monkeys awake,
Offering drinks that taste like a cake.
Dance under stars, but oh, beware,
One might just trip on a plush teddy bear.

So let's laugh more, do pirouettes of fun,
In this dreamscape realm, every night's a run.
With imagination, let's giggle and play,
For tomorrow's reality can wait for the day!

Shimmering Reflections on Water's Edge

The lake mirrors antics, a splendid show,
As frogs in tuxedos put on quite a glow.
They croak out jokes, with such flair and style,
I can't help but chuckle at their witty guile.

Ripples dance and giggle away,
Splashing my shoes, oh what a display!
The fish flip flops, in glimmering delight,
Practicing dives as they take flight.

Fireflies twinkle, a lantern parade,
While I try to waltz with my ice cream fade.
It drips on my shirt, I laugh at the mess,
What a shimmering story, I must confess.

Let the night sparkle, let the fun begin,
With laughter and jokes, like a whirl of spin.
So here at the edge, where all dreams collide,
We'll keep making memories, with the moon as our guide!

Firefly Waltz Under the Canopy

In the dark, they blink and glow,
Little dancers put on a show.
Flapping wings, a silly flight,
Chasing tails in sheer delight.

Bamboo bends with every sway,
Laughing leaves join in the play.
One smooth twirl, a wayward spin,
In this hustle, where to begin?

Giggling frogs leap from a log,
Winking stars play hide and fog.
Moonbeams bounce, a jolly crew,
While crickets sing in laughable tune.

The night wears its best disguise,
With fireflies as painted pies.
Who needs sleep? Let's chase this spree,
In this dance, we're wild and free!

Hidden Rhythms of the Night

Beneath the trees, they twitch and sway,
Bugs in suits, they rave away.
Beetles, ants, with shoes askew,
They conquer floors, it's quite the view.

Chirping crickets, jazzing their song,
Join a band that hums along.
With every beat, they slide and glide,
A wacky soirée, there's no need to hide.

An owl hoots with perfect flair,
Did that leaf just have a tear?
What's this move? The night is young,
Even the trees feel like they've sprung!

Under stars that laugh out loud,
This merry crowd, so free and proud.
Twilight wraps its silly grace,
In this rhythm, we find our place.

Perfumed Air of Midnight Bliss

The scent of flowers playing tricks,
Wafting softly, little kicks.
A heady mix of night and cheer,
It's getting wild around here!

Nectar sippers take a sip,
Their tiny buzz gives quite a grip.
With pollen hats and paths so neat,
They dance on air, can't feel their feet!

The moonbeams giggle, slip and slide,
As breezes turn on joy and pride.
Petals pirouette in the dark,
Chasing scents with a jovial spark.

What's that? A scent of prankish fun,
Whiffs of laughter, every one!
This midnight feast, oh what a bliss,
A fragrant joke we can't dismiss!

Serpentine Shadows of the Shore

Waves creep softly with a laugh,
Tickling toes and snapping gaff.
Stars sprinkle secrets in the spray,
As shadows twist and start to play.

Sandy feet and slippery tricks,
Caught in games that nature picks.
The crab scuttles, shows its moves,
Declaring victory as it grooves.

Moonlight forms a disco ball,
Bouncing off the ocean's call.
Let's surf the night on laugh and cheer,
With sandy wigs, the costumed gear!

When shadows coil like happy eels,
They dance and wiggle, what a meal!
In this party, let spirits soar,
As joy rolls in from the shore!

Echoes of the Whispering Waves

The ocean hums a silly tune,
While crabs dance under the bright moon.
A dolphin wears a party hat,
And waves hello to a curious cat.

Stars wink as they spill their light,
And fish sing karaoke all night.
Seaweed sways like it's in a trance,
While turtles try to learn to dance.

An Evening's Caress

The breeze is playful, it pulls my hair,
A parrot squawks, 'Try not to care!'
Each coconut falls, a comic surprise,
As I dodge them with wide-open eyes.

Laughter bubbles from the salty foam,
While crabs stage a show, far from home.
Balloons tied to a palm tree high,
Waving at clouds drifting by.

Dance of the Fireflies

Fireflies twirl in a dazzling dance,
As frogs in tuxedos try their chance.
With cicadas snoring to keep the beat,
A lizard struts with its tiny feet.

Lightning bugs call out, 'Join the fun!'
While geckos slip, but don't quite run.
Tickling the night with glowing cheer,
As we all laugh, there's nothing to fear.

Beneath the Glistening Veil

Under the net of stars so bright,
A hammock swings with all its might.
A squirrel tries to steal some chips,
While gulls perfect their dance moves and flips.

Banana peels slip under feet,
As laughter blends with the waves' heartbeat.
A misplaced drink brings a splash and giggle,
In this wild place with a whimsical wiggle.

Moonlight's Caress on the Horizon

When the light sneaks in so sly,
All the crabs wear hats, oh my!
They dance around, limbs all akimbo,
Joking with fish, plotting to limbo.

The breeze tells jokes that make us snort,
While the stingrays play a game of court,
One wears glasses, looking all smart,
And the dolphins join in, playing their part.

Listen closely, a parrot will squawk,
Saying, 'Keep it down, I'm trying to talk!'
While coconut drinks pour over the sand,
Every sip feels like a magic wand.

In the moon's glow, laughter takes flight,
As the world spins in joyous delight,
With a twist of fate and a splash of cheer,
We'll keep dancing until dawn is near.

Serenading the Stars Above

There's a crab with a ukulele, quite bold,
Strumming tunes that are funny, not old.
Singing to stars in a quirky key,
Even the fish start to giggle with glee.

The moon takes a bow, a dapper knight,
In a tuxedo made from beams so bright.
He trips over waves, but with style and grace,
Winking with charm, all over the place.

With coconuts clapping, they join in the fun,
Making rhythms that spark just like sun,
As night creatures chuckle, each note is a treat,
This serenade makes our hearts skip a beat.

When the sea turtles say, 'That's quite a tune!'
The octopuses dance, holding a balloon,
Under a sky where the laughter flows,
A funny remembrance as the evening glows.

Silhouettes Under the Glimmering Vault

The silhouettes sway like palm trees in flight,
With a crab in a top hat, oh what a sight!
They're practicing moves for an ocean ballet,
Spinning and twirling in a laborious way.

The starfish judge with a serious face,
Pleased with the rhythms of this underwater race,
Each twirl gets a cheer, a splash and a shout,
While the jellyfish jive, with glow all about.

With sea cucumbers cheering in delight,
They say, 'Keep it going, you're doing just right!'
As the moon lights the stage in a shimmering hue,
The night wraps around us, like an old shoe.

This party of laughter, of feet that can't trip,
Where even the clams join in for a dip.
A twist of the night, with chuckles abound,
In the ocean's embrace, a merrier sound.

Nightfall's Waltz on Coral Reefs

In the reef where the jelly drinks tea,
The lobsters gossip about the sea spree.
With sassy remarks and bubbles they blow,
The party's a riot, with laughter in tow.

The clownfish parade in colorful style,
With rainbow confetti, they dance for a while.
Swirling their tails in a synchronized dance,
Making a splash, they take every chance.

The seaweed sways, trying to join in,
But one little eel thinks it's a sin!
Proposing a contest of wobble and sway,
As the seahorses giggle, in their own way.

Oh, the moonlight brings joy in waves of delight,
As the night turns absurd in playful insight,
With fish in a frenzy and reefs all aglow,
The laughter continues, the joyments grow.

A Melody of Shadows

Beneath the stars, where whispers play,
Crickets sing in a silly ballet.
The moon, a lamp, in its gentle groove,
Makes the fireflies cha-cha and move.

Laughter dances with the cool breeze,
As the coconut falls with an awkward sneeze.
Palm trees sway like they're in a trance,
While the waves join in, eager to prance.

A parrot squawks jokes from its leafy throne,
While a raccoon tries to borrow my phone.
In this wild place, where the fun's never tight,
Even the shadows have parties at night.

So let's toast to the goofy and the strange,
Where the stars seem to giggle, and nothing's arranged.
Raise your glass, give a wink, and take flight,
In this merry realm of mischief and light.

Secrets Win the Night

Under the stars, secrets spill,
Like a pot of beans with a comedic thrill.
The palm trees lean in, they want to hear,
Jokes about crabs and a silly deer.

A mango drops, but it slips with a grin,
As if it knows it's about to begin.
A sea turtle's wisdom, outdated but bright,
Says laughter's the key to a wild, wacky night.

The ocean waves boast of tales and dreams,
Of surfing cats and marshmallow themes.
As the breeze whispers punchlines through my hair,
Even the moon chuckles, floating up there.

So gather around, let your guffaws ring,
As the crickets ad-lib, the air their fling.
With every fun shadow that leaps and spins,
We'll cherish the chaos; that's how fun wins.

Under the Dreamweaver's Gaze

In a world where fish wear tiny hats,
And the moon is known for its quirky chats.
The stars wear sunglasses, looking so bright,
While dolphins practice their stand-up tonight.

A breeze pulls a prank, ruffles my hair,
As a cheeky monkey sneaks up with a stare.
He tosses a pineapple, misses by inches,
And giggles aloud at his own little glitches.

The night wraps around with a whimsical tune,
As the owls hoot softly, making fun of the moon.
Fireflies twinkle like a disco ball,
Inviting all critters to the grandest of all.

So let's join the revelry of smiles and jest,
Where each giggle lingers, and laughter's the quest.
Under the gaze of fantasy's delight,
We'll dance with the shadows, embracing the night.

Ephemeral Glow

A glow from the sea brings laughter near,
As crabs play cards, sipping on root beer.
The turtles cheer with claps and flaps,
While seagulls tell tales of ancient mishaps.

The coconut palm sways, it's quite the tease,
While a breeze swaggers by like it owns the trees.
I tell a joke, it lands with a thud,
But all join in, and we're caught in the flood.

The night's soft whispers create silly dreams,
Of friendly fish plotting wild schemes.
As the stars twirl about in a cosmic ballet,
All revelers chuckle at the fun, come what may.

So let's raise a toast to the night's warm breath,
Where humor is boss, and laughter won't rest.
For in this fleeting glow, as we frolic and play,
We find joy, ever bright, come what may.

Caressed by Night Hues

Underneath those glowing lights,
A toaster danced in cozy sights.
With mango hats and coconut shoes,
They shuffled past the laughing snooze.

The shadows tried their best to tease,
But tripped on jelly, dropped with ease.
A parrot laughed, it made a fuss,
As everyone joined in the bus.

The moon giggled, played peek-a-boo,
While fish wore ties and did the hula,
Chasing dreams in a wobbly boat,
With jellybeans afloat to gloat.

As stars play charades, each a prank,
The night slipped by, a giddy prank.
In this realm of cheer and glee,
Who knew dusk could be so free?

Conversations with the Stars

The stars were gossiping so loud,
While clouds wore shades, looking proud.
One claimed to have a sizzling tale,
About a fish who tried to sail.

The moon raised brows, sipping tea,
Eggplant jokes from Jupiter's spree.
Pineapple jokes were all the rage,
Even Venus burst from her cage.

They spoke of comets, dances spry,
With one on top of a pie in the sky.
Sharing laughs that echoed bright,
While marshmallows lounged in pure delight.

"Oh, chocolate cakes!" one star declared,
As evening twinkled, wide-eyed and bared.
In this cosmic chat, so carefree,
It seemed the universe held the key!

Mirage of Twilight

In the midst of a dance so light,
A crab wore slippers, ready to fight.
Rabbits waltzed and did a spin,
While blowing bubbles with the wind.

The horizon tipped its hat to the crows,
As cucumber blasts burst in colorful flows.
A pineapple twirled, as the sun dipped low,
In a swirl of laughter, putting on a show.

The dusk called out for a chorus grand,
With seagulls strumming on the sand.
This mirage danced with a wink and a tease,
While lizards giggled at the breeze.

As darkness fell, they twirled in joy,
With every shadow, a silly ploy.
In this land of whimsy, how they'd shine,
As twilight scurried with laughter divine!

A Ballet of Waves

Waves pirouetted, taking a bow,
As crabs formed a line, what a show!
With barnacle hats and giggles galore,
The seaweed chanted, "Give us more!"

A dolphin led with perfect grace,
While sea cucumbers kept up the pace.
In a ballet under a shimmering dome,
Each splash an echo, calling the foam.

The moon in the corner, sipping its drink,
Championed the antics, making waves think.
With starfish clapping and singing odd tunes,
While an octopus danced with mismatched shoes.

As tides took turns, a merry sight,
Frogs in a chorus joined in delight.
In this frothy grand, where spirits played,
Who knew that oceans could throw a parade?

Night's Blossoming Muse

Under the stars, the crabs do dance,
With sideways moves, they take their chance.
A parrot squawks, thinking he's cool,
While a dolphin shows off, making waves in the pool.

The moon grins wide, a cheeky glow,
As islanders play limbo low.
Coconut drinks spill with each twist,
A palm tree laughs, it can't resist.

Laughter echoes, the mosquitoes buzz,
One bites a toe, 'Oh, that's a fuss!'
Flip-flops fly as the fun gets loud,
Under the watch of a blushing cloud.

The night winds whisper with playful tease,
As crickets join in with a hum that frees.
In the chaos, sleep plays hide and seek,
While the stars nod gently, 'Tis a wild week!'

Sonnet of the Sea Breeze

A gentle breeze stirs up the fun,
As sea turtles race, trying to outrun.
Jellyfish jive, in a playful parade,
While mermaids giggle, their plans well laid.

The sand is warm, like a hug from the sun,
But watch your step, or you'll find a bun!
For buried treasures sometimes lie,
Like a flip-flop, oh my, oh my!

Seagulls squawk, claiming their dish,
Booty of fries? That's a noble wish!
A beach ball bounces, hitting a guy,
Who stumbles and falls, gives a hopeless sigh.

Yet, laughter rings out, as friends lend a hand,
Together they rise, together they stand.
In breezy nights, fun's our captain true,
With giggles and surf, and skies so blue.

Twilight's Gentle Hand

As twilight falls, the flip-flops fly,
While party lights twinkle, oh my, oh my!
A beach bonfire crackles with cheer,
And the scent of s'mores is ever so near.

The waves join in with a foamy clap,
While silly socks slip in a mishap.
Fishermen joke, their nets turned inside-out,
As they laugh at the fish that swim about.

A hula dancer twirls, spins like a top,
While a goat on the corner claims to be pop!
In the corner, a cat takes a strut,
With swagger so bold, he thinks he's a nut.

Under cosmos bright, antics abound,
As the night unfolds, silly joys are found.
So embrace this charm, let your worries go,
For laughter is golden, like a star's gentle glow.

Soft Reflections Under Stars

Beneath the stars, a turtle winks,
While seaweed shakes, as everyone thinks.
The fishermen tell tales of their catch,
But it's really just bait that was mixed and matched.

In the lagoon, a raft drifts by,
While a lizard tries to catch a pie.
Bamboo chimes make a soft tinkle sound,
As a clumsy crab fumbles round and round.

The moon peeks down, like a cheeky spy,
As little shrimp gather, oh my, oh shy!
With each splash and giggle, they sing and dance,
While fireflies twinkle, caught in a trance.

So let's raise our cups to this joyous night,
With silly moments basked in starlight.
In laughter we find the unwinded art,
Of knowing life's best when it plays its part.

A Dance with Nocturnal Spirits

Underneath the stars that shine,
A group of raccoons on a line.
They twirl and spin, they laugh and prance,
A furry party, a wild dance!

The owls watch in bewildered cheer,
As the night comes alive with cheer.
They hoot and hoot, but just for fun,
We'll dance all night until we run!

In this moonlit circus, they play,
As fireflies join in the fray.
A glow like laughter fills the air,
Nature's party—beyond compare!

So join the fun, don't sit and stare,
Just grab a partner, don't you dare.
Let's break the rules, let's dance a bit,
Under the stars, let's never quit!

Moonlit Sandcastles

Down by the shore with buckets in hand,
We build our kingdom of dreams in the sand.
A castle so grand, with turrets and moats,
But the tide comes in, oh, what a joke!

A crab takes a throne, with a crown made of weed,
While seagulls wail, oh yes, they bleed.
With laughter we run as the waves crash and tease,
"Faster!" we shout, "Please, oh please!"

The moon shines bright on our sandy retreat,
As fish parade by in their finned little fleet.
We slide and we slip in this slippery game,
What's yours is mine, oh, aren't we the same?

One last splash, then off to retreat,
Chasing our dreams in the night so sweet.
Tomorrow we'll build, that's the plan,
For now, we retreat, all covered in sand!

Murmurs from the Underbrush

In the garden where shadows creep,
A chorus of critters begin to peep.
The frogs are croaking their nighttime song,
But the crickets hum along, all night long!

The hedgehogs tumble, the squirrels peek,
Worried and fuzzy, they speak a cheek.
"What's that noise?" asks a startled hare,
"It's just the moon, don't give a scare!"

With glowing eyes, the fireflies wink,
They giggle and twinkle, oh, what do you think?
"Let's throw a rave and dance for a bit!"
What fun to party in this leafy pit!

So grab a leaf, let's sway and play,
Under the stars, we'll be wild and gay.
Murmurs and laughter, a magical night,
Who knew the dark could feel so right?

Captured in Night's Embrace

The moon peeks down with a knowing grin,
While kittens frolic, oh, where to begin?
They chase their tails in a frenzied whirl,
As starlight shines on each ruffled curl.

Lizards lounge on rocks, dressed to impress,
Playing poker, oh what a mess!
"Two pair!" one shouts, with a flick of the tail,
As the night winds dance to a whimsical gale.

An iguana suits up in a tiny bow tie,
While the crickets sing, "Let's give it a try!"
They shimmy and shake in the cool night air,
What a sight for the critters who dare!

So here we are, spirits running free,
In this wild party, come dance with me.
Captured in laughter, in nature's grand space,
Under the night's warm and silly embrace!

www.ingramcontent.com/pod-product-compliance
Lightning Source LLC
Chambersburg PA
CBHW072221070526
44585CB00015B/1433